Finding CONNECTION Within

Mee-Gaik Lim, Ph.D.

BALBOA.PRESS

A DIVISION OF HAY HOUSE

Balboa Press books may be ordered through booksellers or by contacting:

Balboa Press
A Division of Hay House
1663 Liberty Drive
Bloomington, IN 47403
www.balboapress.com
844-682-1282

Because of the dynamic nature of the Internet, any web addresses or links contained in this book may have changed since publication and may no longer be valid. The views expressed in this work are solely those of the author and do not necessarily reflect the views of the publisher, and the publisher hereby disclaims any responsibility for them.

The author of this book does not dispense medical advice or prescribe the use of any technique as a form of treatment for physical, emotional, or medical problems without the advice of a physician, either directly or indirectly. The intent of the author is only to offer information of a general nature to help you in your quest for emotional and spiritual well-being. In the event you use any of the information in this book for yourself, which is your constitutional right, the author and the publisher assume no responsibility for your actions.

Any people depicted in stock imagery provided by Getty Images are models, and such images are being used for illustrative purposes only.
Certain stock imagery © Getty Images.

Print information available on the last page.

ISBN: 979-8-7652-3081-7 (sc)
ISBN: 979-8-7652-3082-4 (e)

Library of Congress Control Number: 2022912099

Balboa Press rev. date: 07/14/2022

Acknowledgments

To my nieces and nephews who have enriched my life
with lessons of patience and acceptance.

Contents

1

Successful Ways to Ask for What We Want

People generally don't assert themselves because they are not familiar with asking for what they want. Asking for what you want is uncomfortable for most people. It may have led to arguments or rejection in the past; hence, it's easier for people to take the path of least resistance and avoid making waves in their relationships.

Since it takes courageous effort to voice our needs, we may fall into the habit of putting our feelings, thoughts, and interests on hold for fear of being turned down or rejected. Not expressing ourselves openly and honestly may eventually lead to resentment and may also hinder our ability to be transparent and voice ourselves freely in relationships.

Our inability to openly ask for what we want may be due to the fact that we did not see our parents openly express themselves. They saw their parents complain about the behaviors of others rather than clearly express their own needs. Parents may complain about the annoying behaviors of their children or spouse rather than ask in clear, simple, constructive ways.

We tend to model the behaviors of those around us. As Jack Canfield stated, "We are an average of six to eight people we hang out with." Since we didn't see our parents model constructive ways of asking, we too may fall into the complaining trap rather than engaging in transparent expression.

Another hesitancy factor may come from our fear of imposing on and inconveniencing others. We may have grown up with the message that our job is to help others, and we may believe it's selfish to ask for what we need. Eventually, after hearing this repeatedly, we learn to put our needs on hold and pause our interests and desires. This negative self-chatter may cause us to continually put our needs, desires, and passions on hold.

To successfully ask for what you want, you need to learn to state your requests in positive ways. Open your statement with an "I" and finish with a positive request. There should be *two positives* in your sentence. When statements are expressed positively, they set you up for success, and people are more likely to cooperate and comply. Most people want to work together and cooperate, not defy and resist. When you openly express your thoughts and needs, you give others opportunities to cooperate, and you also steer them in constructive directions.

Examples:

- I appreciate it when you do your homework before playing on the iPad.
- It helps me when you complete your chores before going to your friend's house.
- It means a lot to me when we spend one-on-one time together each evening.

In asking and expressing yourself, learn to lean in with courageous energy. Whatever emotions you experience, lean into them, and don't run from them. As an adult, model healthy ways to ask. This allows your children to watch you, and likewise, they will use this tool to ask or express themselves with their friends. It also provides them with a successful tool set in their adult years.

Here are some sentence stems to make requests openly and directly. These stems can be used with your spouse, partner, colleagues, children, or friends. These sentence stems steer you to make requests in positive ways.

Reflection Ponderings

I really appreciate it when you_____

_____

_____

_____

I am looking for us to _____

_____

_____

_____

I would like to see us _____

_____

_____

_____

I am interested in _____

_____

_____

_____

I am invigorated when _____

_____

_____

_____

I am encouraged when we _____

_____

_____

_____

I am grateful for your efforts to _____

_____

_____

_____

I am touched by your effort to _____

_____

_____

_____

I value our ability to _____

_____

_____

_____

It is important to me_____

_____

_____

It helps me when you _____

_____

_____

_____

It hurts me when _____

_____

_____

_____

It means a lot to me when _____

_____

_____

_____

It motivates me when _____

_____

_____

_____

I feel connected when you _____

_____

_____

_____

I feel heard and validated when _____

_____

_____

_____

I feel respected when you _____

_____

_____

I feel special when you _____

_____

_____

_____

I feel supported when you _____

_____

_____

_____

When we work together, I feel _____

_____

_____

_____

When you hear me, I feel _____

_____

_____

_____

When you are attentive to my needs, I feel _____

_____

_____

_____

When you take time to _____

_____

_____

_____

Given time, I would like to _____

_____

_____

To strengthen my confidence, I would like _____

_____

_____

_____

To start healing, I would like to _____

_____

_____

_____

Some of the feelings I am struggling with are _____

_____

_____

_____

Your mindfulness motivates me to _____

_____

_____

_____

The privilege of a lifetime is to become who you truly are.

– Carl Jung

Accompanying YouTube Video: https://www.youtube.com/watch?v=9G9J-csLDA8

2

How to Handle Reactive and Explosive Behaviors

Reactive and explosive behaviors are common in partner and family relationships. With little provocation, an individual may fly off the handle and respond with over-the-top fits of explosive rage. Reactive responses are often in the form of a desire to get back at someone and return a punch with a punch. Unfortunately, many people spend much of their time in this reactive response.

Reactive and explosive patterns are rooted in secondary emotions like anger, fury, rage, irritation, annoyance, infuriation, and exasperation. The reactive brain is reptilian and stony in nature. People perceive loss of control and want to avoid harm, so they seek to restore a sense of safety to protect themselves. It's common for people to fall into reactive traps and continually use this preset template to deal with challenging, tense situations. Reactive responses are common in many types of relationships, including those we have with romantic partners, family members, or coworkers.

Consider the case of Maryann.

> When my feelings are misconstrued, misunderstood, and ignored by my spouse, I feel hurt, disregarded, overlooked, and discounted. This eventually creates resentment, anger, and bitterness in me, and I use punishment to get back at my spouse for discounting me and for the pain they inflicted on me.
>
> I now see you as a person who is careless, disregarding, and out to hurt me. Additionally, since you do not have my best interests at heart, I see you as my opponent, and I immediately revoke trust, withdraw from the relationship, and protect myself.
>
> To defend myself and safeguard my well-being, I lash out, attack, shut down, cut you off, ice you out, and eventually disengage from the relationship. When resorting to this vengeful coping, I eventually end up feeling disappointed, defeated, discouraged, disheartened, and alone.

As you see, the reactive and explosive response is disengaging and disconnecting.

If you reflect on this responding behavior, individuals tend to replicate their parents' reactive, disconnecting communication styles. They may have seen their parents react and respond by using disconnecting strategies like attacking or lashing out. Instead of replicating these unproductive patterns, though, it's critical to learn to be vulnerable and express the primary emotions of hurt, sadness, fear, or shame rather than use explosive attacks to respond.

The following personal growth questions can help you examine your reactive behaviors.

Reflection Ponderings

When were some times you felt misunderstood by your partner/spouse?

_____

_____

_____

_____

_____

What feelings did you experience when you were misunderstood?

_____

_____

_____

_____

_____

When you withdraw and disconnect from the relationship, what self-talk do you replay in your head?

_____

_____

_____

_____

_____

In protecting and withdrawing from the relationship, what wounds are you nurturing?

_____

_____

_____

_____

_____

How did it impact you when you saw your parents disconnect from their relationship?

_____

_____

_____

_____

_____

In times of tension, what similarities do you draw between the way your parents coped and the way you cope?

_____

_____

_____

_____

_____

How is being misunderstood by your spouse similar to being misunderstood by your parents?

_____

_____

_____

_____

_____

How did your parents' disengagement and disconnection impact you?

_____

_____

_____

_____

_____

Start to grieve the loss of being ignored, unheard, and misunderstood. It is critical to teach clients to be vulnerable and to express their primary emotions of hurt, sadness, fear, or shame rather than use explosive attacks to respond.

The emotion that can break your heart is sometimes the very one that heals it.

– Nicholas Sparks

Accompanying YouTube video: https://www.youtube.com/watch?v=jKlVscw1gyY

3

Words That Can Implement Change in Your Life

It's easy to slip into a humdrum, complacent routine and remain stagnant in life. While unhappy in their unproductive cycles, many find it challenging to muster up energy to implement changes or steer themselves into constructive changes. Additionally, many people get caught up in stating changes negatively, and this negative self-talk keeps them from making changes or moving forward. When making constructive changes in our lives, it helps to state the changes we desire in positive ways.

The key to change is continually examining our attitudes and learning to express change in desired terms. In doing so, we train ourselves to think in progressive, affirmative ways. Changes stated in positive, directional terms often lead to small, progressive changes. Repetitive, continual practice helps us switch and alter our thought patterns into doable steps.

Consider the following change statements, and try to implement these kinds of adjustments in your conversations.

Instead of saying, *Communication with my husband is intense and conflictual.*

Replace it with, *I would like to communicate clearly and calmly with my husband.*

Instead of saying, *I am struggling with disconnection with my mother.*

Replace it with, *I would like to build deeper connections with my mother.*

Instead of saying, *I am frustrated with frequent tension in my home.*

Replace it with, *I want more peace, calm, and serenity in my home.*

We plant seeds of behavioral change when we state empathic responses in desired, positive behavioral terms. When new behavioral words are introduced, we will eventually make changes that moves us in our desired directions.

The following are some examples of how you can alter negatively expressed statements to statements that bring about change.

Negative: I don't want to be argumentative and confrontational with my wife.
Positive: I want to express myself and my thoughts calmly and clearly to my wife.

Negative: I don't want to be depressed anymore.
Positive: I want to cope and deal with my challenging feelings.

Negative: I do not want to live a fearful and anxious life.
Positive: I want to live life with certainty and courage.

Negative: I don't want to feel timid about the way I live.
Positive: I want to live life with more confidence and self-assurance.

Negative: I don't want to let fear and defeat dominate my life.
Positive: I would like to have more courage and calm assurance in my daily life.

Negative: I want to remove self-doubt from my decisions.
Positive: I want to live life with clarity and firm self-belief.

Negative: I want to reduce my negative, distrustful attitude.
Positive: I want to have trusting, believing, and positive attitudes about people.

Negative: I don't want to be overprotective of my children.
Positive: I want to parent in trusting and supportive ways.

Negative: I want to stop yelling at my children when I'm angry.
Positive: When things get intense at home, I want to talk to my children calmly.

Negative: I don't want to isolate when I feel down.
Positive: I want to reach out and express my struggles to others when I feel down.

Negative: I don't want to ignore my self-care habits.
Positive: I want to be more in tune and give priority to my self-care habits.

Negative: I don't want to resist change.
Positive: I want to use courage to cope with change.

Negative: I want to stop smoking.
Positive: I want to start living a healthy lifestyle.

Again, the key to change is continually examining your attitude and learning to state changes in desired terms. In doing so, you train your brain to think in progressive, affirmative ways, which in turn will help you look for alternative behaviors that support these changes.

*Growth is the process of responding
positively to change.*

— Paul Harvey

Be the change you wish to see in the world.

— Ghandi

Accompanying YouTube video: https://www.youtube.com/watch?v=2iLsMMkWLtY

4

Practical Steps to Increase Happiness in Your Life

It's common for people to get caught up in humdrum routines of life and spend their days completing mundane, unfulfilling tasks. There could be a low-grade level of dissatisfaction and emptiness because their lives are not aligned with their personal desires, goals, and passions.

Many people long to live meaningful, satisfying, enriched lives but are unsure about how to achieve them. Consider simple, practical steps to help you gain personal fulfillment and happiness in your life.

1. Listen to Your Inner Voice

To begin with, don't numb your emotions, mute your voice, censure your thoughts, or frown upon your own interests. When your emotions, ideas, passions, and thoughts are numbed and anaesthetized, resentments will grow and fester. You will feel unimportant if you are repeatedly discounted and disregarded by family members. You begin to think you don't matter, and you shrink your ideas and thoughts as an adult. After years of self-muting, it may rob you of your own happiness, emotional well-being, and peace of mind. When this happens, you may start to keep an emotional tally of how you are discounted and disregarded.

If this becomes a common practice in your relationship, hostility and resentments will grow and it will also lead to distancing behaviors between you and your partner or you and your child. And at times, explosive outbursts may occur over minor issues.

2. Be in Tune with Your Emotions

To increase your personal happiness, it's important to start to be in touch with your own emotions and learn to identify what you are feeling or thinking. Make it your responsibility to express your emotions and thoughts clearly, honestly, and appropriately. Do not hold other people responsible for your own happiness or farm it out to others to make you feel happy or fulfilled. When you experience a certain emotion, thought, or desire, learn to express it rather than mute it.

- **Start to express yourself.**

For example, at work you might use courage to express yourself.
I felt important when you recognized my efforts on the project.
It helps me when you focus on my accomplishments rather than my mistakes.

- **Start to state what you prefer.**

Example:

I really prefer to have a small, private Christmas celebration at our house with our children rather than driving eight hours to celebrate Christmas at my parents' house.
My preference is to complete my current projects before taking on new assignments. I would like to successfully complete the current projects.

- **Start to express your appreciation.**

Example:

It meant a lot to me that you reached out to our son when he lost a soccer game.
It really helps me out when you help the children with their homework.

3. **Avoid Seeking Others' Approval and Acceptance**

Due to the fear of displeasing others, people may compromise their interests and roles in life. Some spend good bits of their lives seeking love, approval, and acceptance from their parents or other significant people.

When you're consumed and powered by pleasing others, you abandon your true self, betray your interests, and become preoccupied and consumed with approval seeking. Additionally, fear of criticism may lead you to live driven by unconscious loyalty to early childhood messages of doing for others or watching out for others.

Example: You may be trained to be self-sacrificial or to embrace the savior syndrome to gain your mother's or father's acceptance.

This inner, unspoken, self-sacrificing mission may cause you to live life tentatively, riddled with uncertainty and self-doubt; hence, you perpetuate your own insecurity about the mission and passion of your life. Start to examine what you want for your life.

The following statements can help you challenge your loyalty to unhealthy scripts that drain your happiness.

Reflection Ponderings

I rob myself significantly by _____

_____

_____

_____

I have nurtured my own inadequacies by _____

_____

_____

_____

Similar to my history, I have _____

_____

_____

_____

Fear has kept me _____

_____

_____

_____

Self-judgment has kept me from _____

_____

_____

_____

Consumed by my interest in keeping others happy, I have _____

_____

_____

_____

4. Strengthen Personal Approval and Acceptance

Be in tune with who you are. Use courage, excitement, and presence to build your sense of personal fulfillment and contentment. Embrace your growth and claim yourself.

Construct a new template to create your own identity. Focus on creating an identity that is based on personal acceptance. Lean into your own life by using secure energy, and focus on building interests that align with your goals. Use courage rather than fear to face life challenges. Learn to be your own self advocate in order to express your interests, passions, and desires.

The following starter sentences can be used to help you increase your personal happiness.

To be true to myself, I would like to _____

_____

_____

_____

To be in tune with my interests, I would like to _____

_____

_____

_____

To embrace my own growth, I would like to _____

_____

_____

To nurture fulfillment and contentment in my life, I would like to _____

_____

_____

_____

Leaning into courage means that I _____

_____

_____

_____

To advocate for myself, I would _____

_____

_____

_____

Make it your responsibility to express your emotions and thoughts clearly, honestly, and appropriately. Also use courage daily to face life's challenges. Learn to be your own self advocate and express your interests, passions, and desires.

Being attuned to oneself is the foundation
for harmony in all other relationships.

– P Wong

Accompanying YouTube video: https://www.youtube.com/watch?v=X3EhLs4FXBM

5

My Personal Bill of Rights

Connecting to one's personal opinions, thoughts, feelings, and expressions is a new experience for many. While we were given tools to excel and advance academically, intellectually, and professionally, we were not given tools to nurture our unique worth and dignity.

While we were growing up, some of our common rights and truths were slowly stripped away when we lived under the constant shadows of fear, shame, guilt, insufficiency, and inadequacy. When our feelings were continually denied and suppressed, we slowly disconnected and departed from our personal thoughts, emotions, and privileges. Additionally, when we're told to conform and streamline our thoughts, behaviors, and feelings to societal standards, we slowly wander from listening to our inner voices and feelings to being disconnected from our values.

For us to live lives full of courage, it's healthy to nurture, honor, and trust ourselves fully. It's hoped that continual affirmations of our uniqueness will enable us to live congruently and genuinely. It is our responsibility to advocate for ourselves.

Consider the following personal bill of rights and think about how you could apply it to your own life.

Attunement—I have the right to be attuned to myself and validated in my emotions.

Belonging—I have the right to create belonging to my own authentic self.

Connect—I have the right to foster strong connections to my thoughts and feelings.

Devote—I have the right to be devoted to my priorities and interests.

Empower—I have the right to empower myself to enjoy new challenges that stretch my comfort zone.

Forgive—I have the right to forgive myself and relinquish old pain and mistakes.

Gentle—I have the right to be gentle and compassionate with myself for past mistakes.

Honor—I have the right to honor my needs and make myself a priority daily.

Invest—I have the right to invest in my own emotional growth and advancement.

Judicious—I have the right to judiciously exercise my trust in people.

Kind—I have the right to speak kind and gentle words about myself.

Loyal—I have the right to be loyal, steadfast, and dedicated to interests that enhance my growth.

Mindful—I have the right to cultivate mindful awareness and be present and engaged in my undertakings.

Nurture—I have the right to nurture healthy, constructive self-chatter that enhances my growth.

Optimal—I have the right to practice optimal living habits to enhance my physical and emotional wellness.

Protect—I have the right to protect my boundaries and create respectful and trusting interactions.

Quiet—I have the right to quiet and calm my mind and sit with uncomfortable emotions.

Resilient—I have the right to build resilient skills and encounter challenges with courage and flexibility.

Self-directed—I have the right to examine possibilities and opportunities and pursue a self-directed path.

Trust—I have the right to trust, believe, and rely on my instincts.

Unwavering—I have the right to maintain unwavering courage to express my thoughts, morals, values, and point of view.

Valiant—I have the right to live life with valiant determination and courage.

Watchful—I have the right to watchfully restore and increase my emotional awareness and acceptance.

eXonerate—I have the right to exonerate myself for early life lessons of growth.

Youthful—I have the right to maintain a youthful, enthusiastic energy to rejuvenate myself.

Zealous—I have the right to zealously cultivate an attitude of gratitude

You will never be free until you free yourself
from the freedom of your own false thoughts.

– Phillip Arnold

Accompanying YouTube video: https://www.youtube.com/watch?v=zpMMOLLLk-8

6

Constraints of Self-Limiting Thoughts

Many of us constrain ourselves with self-limiting, self-defeating, and self-diminishing thoughts. These nagging voices constantly remind us of our inadequacies. When we immerse ourselves in this corrosive babble, we soon convince ourselves that there is something inherently wrong with us. The stormy gust of false chatter is generally encased in emotional insecurities, self-doubt, fear of disapproval, or fear of rejection. They are commonly rooted in generational, defeating patterns. The impact of these diminishing thoughts can increase guilt, shame, anxiety, compulsive behaviors, or even depression.

The babble inhibits our lives and hinders our emotional growth. It helps to challenge these noisy, nagging voices and learn to liberate ourselves to maximize our personal and professional potential. It helps to quieten these corrosive rants and embrace healthy, nurturing self-talk. Additionally, it will be beneficial to immerse ourselves with new narratives and storylines that embrace courage and bravery in our daily functions.

Here are some common limiting beliefs or negative self-chatter that can diminish how one functions.

I'm not good enough and feel incapable of handling big decisions.

I'm not capable and competent like my friend.

I am uncomfortable speaking up for myself.

I might get discounted if I speak up openly.

I can never match up to people who are bright and talented.

I get anxious and feel overwhelmed when others overpower me.

I lose my voice and become small when tension shows up.

I feel powerless to change because there are so many obstacles in my life.

I let fear dominate my thoughts.

I am immobilized and consumed by guilt and shame.

Consider using the following questions to challenge the self-limiting, self-defeating, and self-diminishing chatter.

Reflection Ponderings

On mutedness or self-silencing:

In what ways did you mute yourself that you saw reflected in one or both of your parents?

_____

_____

_____

_____

_____

How did silencing yourself impact your relationships at home and at work?

_____

_____

_____

_____

_____

What is comfortable and convenient about muting yourself?

_____

_____

_____

_____

_____

What parallels do you see between your father's or mother's mutedness and your own in relationships?

_____

_____

_____

_____

_____

On Feeling Overpowered:

How did your father's overpowering behaviors impact you while you were growing up?

_____

_____

_____

_____

_____

In what ways is your boyfriend or spouse overpowering like your father?

_____

_____

_____

_____

_____

What is comfortable about catering to your father or mother, and where else is this catering behavior showing up?

_____

_____

_____

How would your relationships be different if you made yourself a priority?

_____

_____

_____

_____

On Self-Diminishing Behaviors

What is the importance of limiting and diminishing yourself?

_____

_____

_____

_____

What stands out to you about your history of self-limiting behaviors?

_____

_____

_____

_____

How have you diminished yourself in social relationships?

_____

_____

_____

_____

What parallels do you see between your diminishing behavior and that of your mother or father?

_____

_____

_____

_____

_____

What are some feelings you've experienced when you put limitations on your own life?

_____

_____

_____

_____

_____

How have these self-imposed limitations impacted your parenting?

_____

_____

_____

_____

_____

How have these self-imposed limitations impacted your role at work?

_____

_____

_____

_____

_____

How have these self-imposed limitations impacted your social relationships?

_____

_____

_____

_____

_____

On Self-Abandonment

When did you give up your right to make decisions?

_____

_____

_____

_____

How did giving up your rights impact your life?

_____

_____

_____

_____

How has giving up your rights affected the way you relate to your spouse?

_____

_____

_____

_____

How has giving up your rights affected the way you relate to your coworkers?

_____

_____

_____

What is convenient about giving up your rights in relationships?

_____

_____

_____

_____

_____

What emotions have you used to help stand up for yourself?

_____

_____

_____

_____

_____

How have you nurtured your assertive and independent thoughts?

_____

_____

_____

_____

_____

How might your relationships be different if you shared your thoughts openly and transparently at work?

_____

_____

_____

_____

_____

How might your marital relationship shift if you express yourself honestly and genuinely?

_____

_____

_____

_____

_____

Realize that you have the power to tame and quiet these voices. Make it your priority to embrace healthy, nurturing chatter.

Everything you need is within you, the strength, courage and confidence to change your life. You just need to look within yourself and find it.

– Amanda Ray

Every day you must unlearn the ways that you hold you back. You must get rid yourself of negativity so you learn to fly.

– Leon Brown

Accompanying YouTube video: https://www.youtube.com/watch?v=9zZAUpAy69s

7

Healing of Self-Abandonment

Self-abandonment is common when people continually mute and silence themselves for fear of rejection.

When someone grows up in a home where there are vast amounts of conditional expectations or unpredictable anger and rage, that person remains in a constant state of hypervigilance. One can fall into the blame trap and assume personal responsibility when things do not go accordingly. Without realizing it, they are heavily immersed in guilt and shame cycles that keep them immobilized.

People can keep emotions in check and numb themselves in times of tension. They can also resort to evasiveness. Since compliance and performance were used to gain acceptance and approval, it's easy for people to disconnect from themselves, gauging the temperature in the room and performing according to the standards and expectations of others.

Fearful living can cause people to mask their emotions by putting on a cheerful façade. This robs them of opportunities to be open, honest, and transparent with their thoughts or feelings.

In personal and professional relationships, those people remain guarded and defensive, making it hard for others to connect and get to know them in a personal way. When intense emotions emerge in relationships, they become immobilized and are unable to deal with their intense emotions.

When these individuals become adults, it becomes easy for them to resort to evasive, dodging approaches to relationship challenges. When confronted with intense emotions or challenges, the person:

> ➤ disconnects from emotions and thoughts,
> ➤ runs away from feelings to keep from experiencing hurt and other related feelings,
> ➤ shuts off and detaches from true passion,

- ➤ remains emotionally unavailable,
- ➤ stays in a controlled state to keep from unraveling,
- ➤ succumbs to pleasing others to gain acceptance,
- ➤ displays a happy-family façade, or
- ➤ shuns and skirts around conversations that broach intense emotions.

After decades of empty existence and an unfulfilled life, the person may be ready to liberate him- or herself from overpowering feelings of guilt and shame. To start healing, change may be exhibited at multiple levels.

- ➤ Rather than suppressing my thoughts, it's important that I honor, respect, and sincerely recognize and express them.
- ➤ Rather than discounting my needs, it's important that I invest in myself, make myself a priority, and make decisions in my best interest.
- ➤ Rather than numbing my thoughts and feelings, it's important that I express them with honest transparency.
- ➤ Rather than detach from my true self, it's important that I connect to myself in authentic ways.
- ➤ Rather than display a phony, happy façade, it's important that I become comfortable with using valor to create genuine interactions.
- ➤ Rather than using timid efforts to mask over conflict, it is important that I use courage to directly address conflict and confrontation.
- ➤ Rather than absorbing the toxic blame of others, it is important that I listen with compassion and empathy when others share their intense emotions.

When addressing self-abandonment issues, consider using these reflection questions to heal and restore yourself to wholeness.

Reflection Ponderings

I feel remorseful that I have _____

_____

_____

_____

I regret that I _____

_____

_____

_____

I conveniently use evasive distraction to _____

_____

_____

_____

It is sad that I conveniently _____

_____

_____

_____

Consumed by guilt and shame, I _____

_____

_____

_____

Fear has caused me to _____

_____

_____

_____

To honor and respect my thoughts and feelings, I would like to _____

_____

_____

_____

I would like to liberate myself from _____

_____

_____

To clearly express my decisions, I would like to _____

_____

_____

_____

To interact authentically, I _____

_____

_____

_____

I want to learn to sit with my _____

_____

_____

_____

To connect to my emotions means that I _____

_____

_____

_____

To heal, I would like to _____

_____

_____

_____

To be present for yourself, learn to exercise self-compassion and liberate yourself, honor yourself, respect yourself, and be present for yourself. Invest in yourself, and enrich your life with genuine interactions.

The surest way to lose your self-worth is by trying to find it through the eyes of others.

– Becca Lee

To live with purpose. To say the courageous thing. To celebrate the simple gift. To follow your dreams. This is a happy life.

– Mayland Henry

Accompanying YouTube video: https://www.youtube.com/watch?v=ZK0Laezqmho

8

Keys to Strengthen Personal Authenticity

We are often told that taking care of others is a priority. Whether it's our siblings, parents, or friends, we might feel the happiness of others takes precedence over our own happiness. Additionally, we carry out the belief that we are responsible for offering unending support to friends and family. In our effort to offer unrelenting care and support to others, we readily and conveniently brush aside our own needs and pause them perpetually. After decades of ignoring our needs and depleting our emotional reserves, we feel exhausted.

When you stray and betray your true voice, it diminishes your resilience and increases the likelihood you'll live a fragmented, disjointed, compartmentalized, and uninspired life. Your life becomes role defined scripted to meet expectations of others. In an effort to strengthen your authenticity, it is healthy to acknowledge your personal emotional needs. Make it your responsibility to frequently express your emotions, commitments, and thoughts clearly, honestly, and appropriately.

Additionally, learn to speak from a place of courage. Even if your perspective is unpopular, learn to transparently express your values and principles. Being attuned to your personal voice increases the likelihood of live a connected, enriched, vibrant, and abundant life.

When strengthening personal authenticity, consider using the following sentence stems to express your congruent thoughts.

Reflection Ponderings

A new script for myself is _____

_____

_____

_____

A caring act to implement _____

_____

_____

_____

A fear to overcome _____

_____

_____

_____

I am grateful for my ability to _____

_____

_____

_____

I will mindfully _____

_____

_____

_____

I feel special when _____

_____

_____

_____

I feel important when _____

_____

_____

_____

To be kind to myself, I will _____

_____

_____

To respect myself, I will _____

_____

_____

To strengthen personal attunement, I will _____

_____

_____

_____

To have clarity, I will _____

_____

_____

_____

To be gentle with myself, I can _____

_____

_____

_____

To let go, I will _____

_____

_____

_____

To strengthen self-respect, I will _____

_____

_____

_____

To help me find my voice, I would like to _____

_____

_____

_____

To be authentic, I would like to _____
_____
_____

To be transparent, I would like to _____
_____
_____
_____

To be more present, I would like to _____
_____
_____
_____

To start living genuinely, I would like to _____
_____
_____
_____

To continue to love myself, I would _____
_____
_____
_____

To feel valued, I will _____
_____
_____
_____

To strengthen my voice, I will _____
_____
_____
_____

To validate my feelings, I will _____

_____

_____

To put myself first, I will mindfully _____

_____

_____

_____

With courage, I will _____

_____

_____

_____

With renewed energy, I will _____

_____

_____

_____

With self-assuredness, I will _____

_____

_____

_____

Learn to speak from a place of courage. Make it your responsibility to frequently express your emotions and thoughts clearly, honestly, and appropriately. Being attuned to your personal voice increases the likelihood of living a connected, enriched, vibrant, and abundant life.

Knowing yourself is the beginning of all wisdom.

— Aristotle

**There is nothing more vital to your life than
living an authentic, empowered life.**

Accompanying YouTube video: https://www.youtube.com/watch?v=4BdalBqFz2Q

9

The Dance of Self-Sabotaging Relationships

While people desire love, affection, attention, and intimacy in their primary relationships, they're commonly attracted to partners who are unable to consistently meet those needs. These partners may be emotionally unavailable or may carry equal amounts of unresolved childhood baggage like they do themselves. Most self-sabotaging relationships have strong historical origins from childhood.

Some of the barricades to intimacy are strongly rooted in one's parents' destructive relationship templates. Common relationship configurations include:

- accusatory, dodging interchanges between couples
- constant conflictual clashes
- excessive need for assurance to nurse one's insecurity
- frequent reactive, volatile squabbles
- hypercritical, nitpicking tug-of-war
- the relationship is overrun with antagonist, animosity, ill-feelings
- disconnected, avoidant existence
- retaliatory, tit-for-tat exchanges

Self-sabotaging energy has its origins in home environments where parents are passive, unresponsive, and neglectful. Additionally, extensive history of volatile, toxic exchanges between parents only serves to confirm one's deep-seated feelings of unworthiness or inadequacy.

Common self-sabotaging self-talk includes:

What is it about me that caused my father to leave?
My mother keeps choosing men over me.
I can't do anything right! What's wrong with me?

There must be something wrong with me.
I am not as cool as my friends.
I am not good enough.
I am not slim enough.
I am not pretty enough.
I keep failing. I am not smart like my sister.
Why can't I do anything right?

This empty, gloomy, negative perception sets them on a lonely, self-depreciating, self-rejecting, self-critical emotional trajectory. In significant relationships there may be an unceasing search for affirmative love from their partner or other social relationships. Vast amounts of energy are spent searching for validating confirmation from their partner or from family members.

While there is an unending need for love, the person fears intimacy, fears abandonment, fears connection, and fears being vulnerable. When in relationships, there is a high degree of volatility, and it vacillates between being extremely loving to extremely conflictual. The couple falls into the pursue-distancing cycle.

After a period of calm, loving, engaging connection as a couple, the unconscious self-sabotaging chatter seeps in and triggers conflictual, distancing, score-keeping, retaliatory exchanges. Deep-rooted self-sabotaging tapes get stirred up and remind the person to start distancing for fear of possible rejection or abandonment.

This sets them on a path to replicate the path of their parents' marriage. Common demolishing tactics of blame, suspicion, and attacking now become a comfortable exchange in their relationship. Instead of examining their own toxic, self-defeating chatter, they conveniently transfers blame to their partner and replicates similar self-defeating relationship dynamics as their parents.

Some of them include:

- inflammatory, accusing, blaming fights
- shutting down and isolative stances
- days of silent treatment
- catering, chameleon-like behavior to deter rejection

To reverse these recurring self-sabotaging cycles, it helps to take responsibility for overhauling your destructive thoughts. Examine your fears of abandonment and rejection, and examine how you create conflict to both protect yourself and avoid intimacy.

Instead of succumbing to accusatory, dodging interchanges, learn to have transparent conversations and open dialogue. Communicate to understand rather than communicating to defend your point. Seek to understand the emotions that drive you and your partner's behaviors.

Consider these reflective thoughts:

Is my partner defending his point because he felt blamed?
When attacked, do my partner's defensive behaviors parallel that of his childhood defensiveness?
Is my partner responding because his or her wounds of insecurity are triggered?
Being discounted triggers my partner's self-protective, shut-down, avoidant behavior.

Instead of addressing issues through conflictual attacking, blaming, and finger point, learn to express your own feelings of disappointment, discountedness, defeatedness, or hurt.

Consider these expressions.

I felt unprotected when you defended your mother instead of standing up for me.
I felt discounted when you made independent decisions without asking for my input.
I felt unimportant when you planned out our vacation without asking for my opinion.
I felt unsupported when you overturned my discipline decisions.

Instead of engaging in reactive, volatile squabbles, make it a priority to understand your own emotional triggers. What key emotions from your childhood were ignited and cause you to over-react?

Could it be related to early patterns of being discounted and feeling unimportant?
Could it be related to your fear of rejection?
Could it be feeling overpowered and losing your voice?
Could the putdowns remind you of your early experiences with your dad?

Understanding your own hot buttons may enable you to respond objectively without dredging all conversations through childhood wounds. Also, be in tune to your unconscious desire to hold your partner responsible for meeting unfulfilled childhood needs.

Instead of participating in hypercritical nitpicking, realize you can choose to disengage from power struggles. Decide if you and your partner are caught in a cyclical pursuer-distancing trap that is similar to your parents'. It is critical to learn to engage in calm conversations.

Consider these reflections to break old power struggles.

Reflection Ponderings

Like my parents, I use conflict to _____
_____
_____
_____

I tend to disengage when I feel _____
_____
_____
_____

I get hypercritical when I feel _____
_____
_____
_____

I allow my fear of rejection to _____
_____
_____
_____

When my rejection radar shows up, I _____
_____
_____
_____

I would like to take time to _____

_____

_____

_____

I would like to be better at asking for _____

_____

_____

_____

It is new for me to _____

_____

_____

_____

Learn to quiet your fears, and address them openly. Seek to understand the historical roots of your fears of intimacy, rejection, or abandonment. Start to affirm yourself, and be attentive to your own emotional needs. Create healthy self-talk that surrounds themes of adequacy, sufficiency, and worth.

We can never obtain peace in the outer

world until we make peace with ourselves.

— Dalai Lama

Accompanying YouTube video: https://www.youtube.com/watch?v=-vEuywjeLfk

10

The Importance of Being Present for Yourself

Being present for yourself means there is intentional mindfulness to focus on being in the here and now. It means one's energy is not expended by worrying about past events or future happenings. There is minimal focus on worrying and rumination about the what ifs.

When people are present for themselves, they let go of perfectionist expectations and role-prescribed traps from parents, spouses, or adult children, and they let go of emotionless, mechanical, robotic existences. They do not allow unending need for acceptance to drive their decisions.

Instead, when people are present for themselves, they are comfortable in their own skin, have a clear understanding of themselves, and navigate through life with calm confidence. Energy is spent on celebrating possibilities, potentials, and opportunities. Being in touch with their feelings and thoughts, these people express themselves genuinely and congruently.

Relationships are free of unexpressed obligations, but instead, elements of empathic connection and compassionate understanding drives relationships. In conversations, one person clearly hears others' perspectives with an open mind and is in tune to the interior emotions, thoughts, intentions, and needs of people. He or she is able to differentiate others' emotions without being engulfed by feeling emotionally exhausted.

Life can be a powering-through experience dominated by one competitive experience after another. Time can be spent chasing the next dream, the next goal, the next success, or the next accomplishment. To gain acceptance, a person's agenda is continually documented by external demands and expectations.

Instead, when people are present, they're able to follow their dreams and create paths they have defined for themselves without fear of judgment or repercussions. Being liberated from external pressures to conform and perform, they are able to savor celebratory experiences, treasure daily connections, and enjoy the simple pleasures of life. Being present means they conscientiously work from a place of calm and composure. With personal acceptance, they live satisfied lives filled with contentment, fulfillment, and optimism.

We create expectations and commonly get caught up living a hectic life that adds stress, anxiety, and tension in our life. With accelerated living, we keep on going through to-do lists in our heads, and it keeps us from truly relaxing. Without conscious awareness, we get caught up in a rat race that keeps us perpetually worn out and feeling out of touch with yourself. These expectations may be embedded in fears, like the fear of disappointing others, of being inadequate, or of not measuring up.

When we're present for ourselves, we keep grounded and connected to our beliefs, values, and expectations. We are able to set expectations that match our realities. We are able to liberate ourselves from using performance to measure up or chase competitive drives or continually strive to meet societal expectations. We create personal awareness and function from a place of adequacy, sufficiency, and acceptance. Our worth is defined by who we are—not by how much we perform to meet these imaginary measuring sticks. The focus is to be kind to ourselves and embrace ourselves fully.

Being present for yourself means that you spend energy celebrating possibilities, potentials, and opportunities. You are in touch with your feelings and thoughts and express yourself genuinely, congruently, and freely. You conscientiously work from a place of calm and composure in order to enjoy a contented, fulfilled life.

Being fully in the present, you experience the timeless. In the timeless, you find your true self.

– Deepak Chopra

Accompanying YouTube video: https://www.youtube.com/watch?v=M5lg0A4rxdM

11

The Value of Self-Reflection

Self-reflection is an inner awareness that allows us to look at our thoughts with focus, interest, and curiosity. The intent of self-reflection is to examine our internal dialogues and enhance personal self-compassion and introspection. Self-chatter is common to all of us, and we can use self-reflection to examine the origins of faulty thought patterns and emotions that trigger the negative chatter.

Self-reflection enables us to examine our contributions to tense situations and assume ownership for our roles in the conflicts. When repetitive destructive behaviors persist, it is common for us to ruminate on our faults and fall into self-condemnation. The interest is to address the patterns of unhealthy emotional interactive cycles and learn to respond with constructive emotions.

Introspective self-reflection is essential for personal growth and could lead to changed patterns of thinking that promote happiness and fulfillment. There are multiple benefits of self-reflection. I've listed some below.

Self-reflection:

- allows a person to shift their outlook to create a greater self-connection.
- strengthens empathy and increases attentive listening.
- improves critical thinking and decision-making skills.
- eliminates reactive responses in tense situations.
- enhances proactive, calm responses.
- challenges beliefs and assumptions that inhibit constructive growth.
- helps a person examine self-crucifying, faulty thoughts.
- assists a person in choosing healthy behaviors and thoughts.

The intent of self-reflection is to examine one's internal dialogue and enhance self-compassion and introspection.

*There is no greater journey than the
one that you must take to discover all
of the mysteries that lie within you.*

– Michelle Sandlin

Accompanying YouTube video: https://www.youtube.com/watch?v=LWG4Bup4xBc

12

Chatter of Inadequacy and Insufficiency

The internal chatter of inadequacy and insufficiency is similar to the process of how an oyster makes a pearl. An oyster secretes a microscopic crystal coating that helps form a pearl, and the process can take from a few months to a few years.

The progress of our internal chatter takes years to develop, and it manifests itself in later years. As humans, we have the propensity for self-defeating tendencies, and the formation of these self-inadequacy and insufficiency chatter has its roots in early in childhood.

Here's an example of the developmental process of internal inadequacy and insufficiency chatter.

My early life was peppered with shame, unacceptance, insufficiency, and inadequacy. In elementary and middle school, I felt pressured to be social, to stand up for myself, and to look a certain way—be slim, be chic, be hip, and so forth. Since I didn't fit in, I often felt unaccepted by my peers. The origins of disparaging thoughts of self-criticism and self-judgment started to rattle in my head.

In high school, I felt left out and that I was inadequate, not measuring up because I was not as cool as the other students. This further perpetuated self-deprecating thoughts. With my family I felt blamed, discounted, unheard, misunderstood, and unsupported. It sparked feelings of loneliness, rejection, and inadequacy. My negative chatter spiraled and grew immensely.

Bombarded with decades of disparaging criticisms, I began to see myself as a worthless, insignificant person. I got stuck in a shame-bound silo and was unable to spin out of it. I frequently resorted to feeding my soul with harsh and disparaging chatter. Filled with personal disapproval, I sought to fill my void by pleasing others to gain acceptance and eagerly accommodated to gain a sense of worthiness. Hungry for love, I craved all kinds of attention, even those that were detrimental to my own wellness. I tolerated friends who put me down and belittled me.

Driven by fear of being unloved and unaccepted, I became my own perpetrator and perpetuated negative self-chatter. I was consumed by anger, anxiety, and self-loathing,

In relationships, I farmed out my worth and put it into the hands of family and friends. In my eagerness to please others, I ignored and neglected my own emotional needs. I lost touch with myself and voluntarily:

- abandoned myself.
- discounted myself.
- disregarded myself.
- disrespected myself.
- ignored myself.
- minimized myself.
- neglected myself.
- shrank myself.

Since I readily shrink self and minimize myself, I easily get into a defensive posture and am unable to accept feedback or constructive criticism. It fuels and triggers my shame button from childhood. I respond reactively and either lash out or shut down emotionally to keep from feeling hurt.

In healing from inadequacy and insufficiency, start to define your own identity and learn to express your thoughts, feelings, and perceptions. Get out of the reactionary auto-pilot zone, and learn to express uplifting and invigorating self-chatter. Understand your default triggers and reactiveness to these emotions.

Learn to understand your strong emotions and the historical origins of these emotions. Increased self-awareness may help you select authentic self-chatter that is empowering and not defeating.

Use courage to maintain curiosity about yourself and your interactions. Create a meaningful existence that allows you to congruently express yourself.

To confront feelings of inadequacy and insufficiency, consider using the following sentence stems to help you heal.

Reflection Ponderings

My adequacy caused me to _____

_____

_____

_____

Engulfed by toxic shame, I _____

_____

_____

_____

Feeling insufficient and inadequate, I have _____

_____

_____

_____

I have used self-criticism and self-judgment to _____

_____

_____

_____

In my eagerness to please others, I _____

_____

_____

_____

Immersed in self-loathing, I _____

_____

_____

_____

Having been discounted, it is easy for me to _____

_____

_____

_____

Continual isolation has caused me to _____

_____

_____

Shrinking and minimizing myself has led to _____

_____

_____

_____

Guarded, walled-up living has _____

_____

_____

_____

Hungry for attention, I _____

_____

_____

_____

Living defensively, I _____

_____

_____

_____

Consumed by fear of being unaccepted, I _____

_____

_____

_____

Define your own identity and learn to express your thoughts, feelings, and perceptions. Learn to express uplifting, inspirational, and invigorating thoughts. Use courage to congruently express yourself.

When you are content to be simply yourself and don't compare or compete, everyone will respect you.

– Lao Tzu

Nothing can bring you peace but yourself.

– Ralph Waldo Emerson

Accompanying YouTube video: https://www.youtube.com/watch?v=1-2rV5dXpvU

13

Living Life with Courage

It is easy to fall prey to fear when confronted with challenging, new, or uncomfortable situations. The inclination is to use procrastination, avoidance, and excuses to remain frozen where you are. It helps to understand the grip of fear that keeps you paralyzed.

To live with courage means that you make a conscious choice to step out of your comfort zone to liberate yourself. It takes courage to come out of the shadows and freely express your values, principles, beliefs, passion, interests, intentions, inclinations, preferences, and plans.

Consider various ways to boost and strengthen the energy of courage in your life. Learn to express yourself transparently. Stand by what you say rather than backing down and succumbing to thoughts and decisions of others. You diminish yourself when you cave in and continually acquiesce. We were taught early in life to make our parents proud. We spend vast amount of our lives chasing the dreams, visions, missions, and aspirations of our parents or society. We waste time making things look glossy and acceptable to please others. Learn to express your thoughts and opinion with vulnerability.

The following are some sample statements to get you started with expressing yourself transparently.

Reflection Ponderings

The way I see it is _____

_____

_____

_____

My preferences are _____

_____

It is important to me that I _____

_____

_____

I feel supported when _____

_____

_____

To live life with courage, align your thoughts and feelings with your actions. Nurture your personal passions, opinions, and viewpoints, and take steps to realize them. Stand up for what speaks to your soul, and express it unapologetically. Eliminate sacrificing or foregoing your needs to gain acceptance. Avoid pausing your interests for fear of disappointing others.

Here's an example of congruent living. Due to your demanding work schedule, you have limited time with your family during the weekend. To congruently express yourself, you turn down the invitation to go to a movie with your friends in order to spend quality time with your family.

To live life with courage march to your own tune, express your original thoughts, think for yourself, share your convictions, nurture your awareness, be responsive to persuasions that speak to you, follow your urgings, and celebrate your individuality. It takes little resistance to be a follower. It is easy to fall into the trap of pleasing others to gain acceptance; however, it takes effort and courage to march comfortably to the convictions of your heart. Use bravery to make decisions.

To live life with courage, learn to show up for yourself and protect your time, energy, finances, and well-being. Set firm boundaries for yourself and consistently honor your priorities. Limit your time with people who drain your energy or consume your emotional space unnecessarily. Understand the demands of high-drama friends or family members who will take a toll on you emotionally. It is not your job to make others happy or keep them from feeling unhappy or sad. Realize that the choices they made keep them stuck in life and keep them from moving forward in life. Avoid using compliance, accommodation, and catering to interact in relationships.

To live with courage, view your mistakes as growth opportunities, and learn to cancel out guilt and shame chatter. Remove the chatter of the inner critic that reminds you of the multiple times you have failed. Enjoy your humanity, and make lots of room for forgiveness. Treat your slipups as stepping stones to refine your skills. Also, view these as invaluable lessons to strengthen traits of tenacity and persistency within you. Nurture slipups as opportunities to practice self-kindness and self-compassion.

To live life with courage, respect yourself. Start to appreciate, cherish, value, nurture, and express yourself. When you hear and honor yourself, others will treat you similarly. Consistently stand up for yourself, and do not allow yourself to be manipulated or influenced by others. Learn to acknowledge your needs and express your preferences and opinions rather than denouncing them. Disengage from toxic, disrespectful relationships where individuals continually leech energy from or belittle you.

Consider using these reflection stems to heal and restore courage
and wholeness in your life:

Reflection Ponderings

To stand up for myself, I _____

_____

_____

_____

To live with courage, I would like to _____

_____

_____

_____

With bravery I can _____

_____

_____

_____

To respect myself, I _____

_____

_____

_____

To nurture my awareness, I can _____

_____

_____

Being transparent means that I _____

_____

_____

_____

To celebrate my individuality, I _____

_____

_____

_____

Honoring personal acceptance means that I _____

_____

_____

_____

To claim myself, I can _____

_____

_____

_____

To fine tune respect for myself, I _____

_____

_____

_____

To honor my humanity, I would like to _____

_____

_____

    To live life with courage, liberate yourself from unnecessary limitations in your life. Remove binding chains of oppression, and allow your values to drive your actions and set yourself free. Be attuned to your own vision and mission in life and claim yourself.

Life shrinks or expands in proportion to one's courage.

– Anais Nin

You will never do anything in this world without courage. It is the greatest quality of the mind next to honor.

– Aristotle

Accompanying YouTube video: https://www.youtube.com/watch?v=2egkFc4xx4A

14

The Pitfalls of Self-Judgment

Criticism and judgment clearly weigh us down and continually rob us of our senses of happiness, adequacy, significance, and worth. It is common for individuals to inflict pain on themselves by continually nurturing self-critical thoughts. These judgmental beliefs devalue and rob us of our relationships with ourselves. Decades of self-judgment not only hold us back, but keep us small and weaken our resolve to create the best versions of ourselves.

The following is an example of the way self-judgment impacts one's emotional wellness.

For fear of judgment and criticism, I keep people at arm's length. In relationships, I have the tendency to hang on to feedback from others and habitually dwell on these negative thoughts and get bogged down by them. When I assume that others have negative thoughts about me, I ruminate on these and soon adopt them as personality flaws and readily became *one* with these flaws.

Some of the thoughts that I dwell on include:

- I don't want to call attention to myself.
- I don't want to rock the boat.
- I don't like being the center of attention.
- I don't want to look ridiculous and stupid.
- It is best to keep quiet because I might say the wrong thing.
- I don't want to disappoint my parents or my teachers or my friends.

As a child, I was scared of stepping out of line for fear of being judged and criticized. For fear of saying the wrong thing, I often study a situation, critique it, overanalyze it, and weigh out consequences before I act. I constantly worried that my actions would displease others. I inflated my mistakes and replayed scenarios of minor mistakes and became extremely critical of myself. Additionally, I lived under the constant threat that others would use my mistakes as ammunition against me.

I experience decision paralysis because I assume others will criticize my decisions. I seldom initiate activities or take the lead. In social settings, I depend on others to take the lead so I don't have to deal with criticisms.

I adopted the mission of doing things to make others happy. This state of existence is inhibiting as I set a ceiling on my own happiness. Due to the self-imposed judgment, I miss out on enjoying true freedom and happiness. Life becomes a scripted role rather than connected interaction because most of my relationships were built on fake, surface, and superficial relating.

This defensive dance keeps others from penetrating my shell so I don't have to open up. I wrapped my thoughts around the fear that if others knew my true self, they would not like me. I form my identity around my inadequacies and insecurities. This defensive posture has resulted in living an unfulfilling, empty, and lonely life.

The disconnected stance inhibits me from letting my guard down to be who I am. I get boxed in by my anxious, worried aura. I'm often consumed by self-condemning scripts and allowed them to define me.

To liberate myself, I want to start living for me and acknowledge my own thoughts. Instead of being wrapped up in pleasing others, I want to seek self-acceptance. I want to accept my own humanity and make room for mistakes that enhance my growth. I want to recognize I am a human with emotions and freely liberate myself from oppressive thoughts.

I would like to reduce the chaotic noise in my head and instill a calm, accepting energy within me. The following are examples of self-accepting scripts.

I want to create a new story line that surrounds self-acceptance, security, sufficiency, adequacy, significance, and belonging.

I am interested in using my voice with courage.

It is healthy for me to view my mistakes as opportunities for growth.

I would like to highlight and dwell on my capabilities and strengths.

It is important for me to take responsibility for my own happiness.

I am interested in using liberating energy to relate to others

I want to nurture self-acceptance and self-love.

My priority is to focus on healing my soul.

I want to create space for peaceful, calm existence.

I would like to nurture and be present for myself.

It is important that I make decisions that is in my best interest.

In thinking about reducing the judgmental noise that clangs
loudly within you, consider these stems.

Reflection Ponderings

I want to create space for _____

_____

_____

_____

I like to nurture _____

_____

_____

_____

I am interested in making room for _____

_____

_____

_____

I would like to highlight my _____

_____

_____

_____

With courage, I will _____

_____

_____

_____

Self-liberating thoughts to celebrate are _____

_____

_____

_____

New story lines to build upon are _____

_____

_____

_____

The muscle I want to strengthen is _____

_____

_____

_____

Priorities to cultivate include _____

_____

_____

_____

To liberate yourself, make it a habit to practice compassion, kindness, and consideration. Value your intrinsic worth, and shed more light on your uniqueness. Instead of being wrapped up in pleasing others, create space for personal acceptance and start living for yourself. Accept your own humanity, and make room for mistakes that enhance your growth.

The most terrifying thing is to
accept oneself completely.

– Carl Jung

Self-approval and self-acceptance in
the now are the main keys to positive
changes in every area of our lives

– Louise Hay

Accompanying YouTube video: https://www.youtube.com/watch?v=pwe04cY6o-U

15

How to Overcome Inadequacy and Insufficiency Self-Talk

As mentioned, our internal chatter takes decades to develop and manifests itself in later years. As humans, the propensity for self-defeating tendencies and the formation of these self-inadequacy and insufficiency chatter has its roots in early childhood.

The following are some personal growth questions to challenge these toxic self-chatter.

Reflection Ponderings

What are my default triggers that cause me to respond reactively to my partner?

_____

_____

_____

_____

_____

How has my fear of judgment limited my ability to be who I am?

_____

_____

_____

_____

_____

How have I allowed others' negative self-talk to impact my life?

_____

_____

_____

_____

_____

How have these negative, consuming thoughts impacted my self-worth?

_____

_____

_____

_____

_____

How have I continually nurtured thoughts of inadequacy and insufficiency?

_____

_____

_____

_____

_____

How do I continually shrink myself while empowering others?

_____

_____

_____

_____

_____

How might an increase in awareness help me regulate emotional reactions?

_____

_____

_____

_____

_____

What choices have I made to remain small and intimidated?

_____

_____

_____

_____

_____

When defensive, what am I protecting?

_____

_____

_____

_____

In what ways does my self-chatter parallel that of my parents?

_____

_____

_____

_____

What obstacles have I set to limit my own growth?

_____

_____

_____

_____

If my thoughts, feelings, and behaviors are congruent, what would I express?

_____

_____

_____

_____

_____

If I use honest transparency in relationships, how might I behave differently?

_____

_____

_____

_____

_____

How might working from an empowered emotional space impact my relationships?

_____

_____

_____

_____

_____

What might be some liberating thoughts to strengthen my sense of adequacy?

_____

_____

_____

_____

_____

I hope these questions will help you reevaluate the impact of your historical scripts on your own self-talk. In changing the self-talk, be attentive to your own prescribed limiting chatter. Give yourself permission to rewrite your scripts that transport you back to your true perceptions and values. Listen to internal voices that continually steer you to listen to your passions and preferences.

A priority to implement is to honor yourself by consistently nurturing your emotional adequacy and sufficiency. Continue to strengthen your secure foundation to help you in your personal journey.

*Self-talk is the most powerful form
of communication because it either
empowers you or defeats you.*

– Unknown

*What you tell yourself everyday will
either lift you up or tear you down.*

– Unknown

Accompanying YouTube video: https://www.youtube.com/watch?v=ZHG_WK21DCc

Conclusion

On life's journeys, it's common to be overrun by faulty, restraining beliefs that have derailed you from embracing your goals, interests, and passions. Over time, uncertainty and self-doubt may have gradually crept in and led you to live a self-sacrificing life. In addition to a lethargic attitude, it may be hard to fend off uncalled-for negative self-chatter that inhabits your mental space.

As you consciously find connection within you, may you nurture, honor, and give yourself permission to live a vibrant, fulfilling life. With calm confidence, continually affirm your uniqueness, and be in tune to with your mission in life. Make it your responsibility to be your strongest advocate, and embrace your growth. Make it a daily practice to lean into courageous energy to express yourself. My hope is that this book will inspire you to step out and venture to new heights of growth to find connection within.

Reflective Ponderings

To affirm my uniqueness, I will start to _____

_____

_____

_____

A daily practice to lean into is _____

_____

_____

_____

A new growth venture to undertake is _____

_____

_____

_____

To enrich my life with celebratory moments, I will _____

_____

_____

_____

To find connection within, I will _____

_____

_____

_____

Printed in the United States
by Baker & Taylor Publisher Services